Survivor
by Cathleen Schurr

My Childhood
in Wartime France
by Charles Hipser

Two Memoirs About World War II

Table of Contents

Memoir

What is a memoir?

A memoir (MEM-war) is writing that covers a short period of time in the life of the person writing it. Memoirs focus on the events, thoughts, and feelings of that person. They are often about a specific time or place or a moment in history that is important to the writer. Memoirs communicate the conflict and drama of events as they unfold but with a strong, personal point of view.

What is the purpose of a memoir?

The purpose of a memoir is to describe events as the writer remembers them. These writers want to share their experiences with the rest of the world. Some writers may have lived through important times or contributed to world-changing events. They want readers to know what they did and to share what they felt. Writers may also use the memoir as a journey of self-discovery. Writing about the past can help people better understand themselves and how they came to be who they are.

How do you read a memoir?

When you read a memoir, you are reading a first-person narrative: one person's memory of an event or time. Enter into the moment with the writer. Try to picture yourself there. Think about what is important and why the writer chose to write about the event. Look for insight into why it was important to the writer. The writer remembered the moment in great detail. Will you?

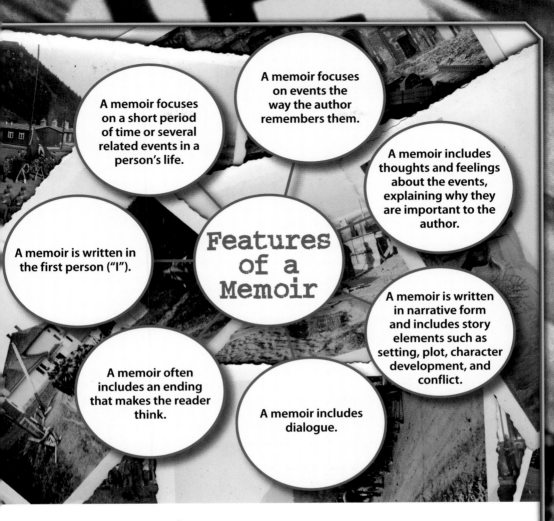

Features of a Memoir

A memoir focuses on a short period of time or several related events in a person's life.

A memoir focuses on events the way the author remembers them.

A memoir includes thoughts and feelings about the events, explaining why they are important to the author.

A memoir is written in the first person ("I").

A memoir is written in narrative form and includes story elements such as setting, plot, character development, and conflict.

A memoir often includes an ending that makes the reader think.

A memoir includes dialogue.

Who writes memoirs?

In the past, people who took part in world-changing events, like explorations or scientific discoveries, wrote memoirs. The writers wanted to give an eyewitness account of the event. But memoirs are not always about major or public events. You don't have to be famous to write a memoir! People today often write memoirs because a period of time in their lives was important to them. Memoirs can be about everyday events. They are interesting to readers because of the way the writer remembers and explains the events.

Tools for Readers and Writers

Writer's Voice

When your friends call you on the phone, can you recognize their voices? Every voice is distinctive, just like each friend's personality. A writer's voice is no different. Everyone's writing is different from everybody else's. Every writer chooses certain topics, words, and details and uses a certain style and mood that make his or her writing as unique as a fingerprint. Good writers use voice to add feeling to their writing. Good writers also adapt, or change, their voices for different audiences and purposes. For example, you would use a different voice to write an e-mail to your cousin inviting him to your soccer game than you would use to write a letter to your principal requesting a field trip for your class.

Suffixes

Good writers use as few words as possible to convey meaning. One way they accomplish this task is by using suffixes. When suffixes are placed at the end of a root or base word, the meaning of that root word changes. For example, the suffix -y means "like" or "having the character of." Instead of saying "being like fruit," authors use *fruity*. Instead of saying "having the character of sun," authors use *sunny*.

Text Structure and Organization

Authors put words together in several ways called text structures, or organizational patterns. These text structures include compare and contrast, cause and effect, problem and solution, sequence of events or steps in a process, and description. In many cases, authors use key words and phrases to help readers determine the text structure being used, but in some cases, readers have to think about the text's structure on their own. Knowing how the author organized the events, ideas, and information in the text helps the reader to understand and remember what was read.

About World War II

World War II, also known as the Second World War, took place from 1939 to 1945. During this time, many of the world's nations were involved in battles across Europe, North Africa, and the South Pacific. Nations participated in the conflict on the side of either the Allied or the Axis nations. The Allied powers included the United States, Soviet Union, England, France, and China. The Axis countries included Germany, Japan, and Italy. Even though different nations entered the war at different times and for varying reasons, World War II became the largest conflict the world has ever known. More than sixty million people died.

The official start of World War II was September 1, 1939. That is the date Germany, led by Adolf Hitler and the Nazi Party, invaded Poland. Two days later, England and France declared war against Germany after it refused to withdraw its troops from Poland. In anticipation of the fighting to come, thousands of people rushed to leave London. While warring against both England and France, Germany entered and occupied more European nations, including France, which it took over in 1940. The United States did not enter the war until late 1941.

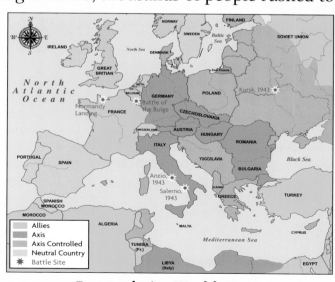

Europe during World War II

Survivor

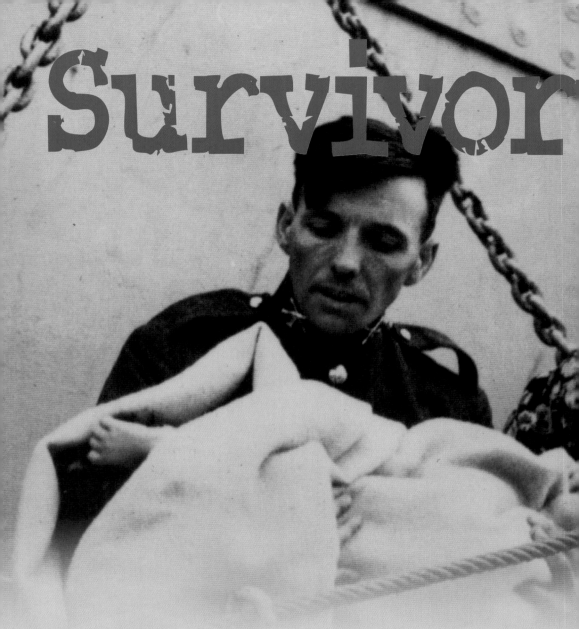

I do not dream about it anymore. Sometimes whole days go by, and I do not even think about it. But then something stirs my memory—pictures of dives to the *Titanic*, an article about the *Lusitania*, an old film about war at sea—and my mind travels back to early September 1939, when World War II began, and especially to the day I almost became a casualty of the war's first submarine attack.

It was almost by chance that I was on board the SS *Athenia*. At the time, I was a twenty-three-year-old American woman working as a secretary in London. My father had been born in London, so it was like my second home.

This is me in 1939 shortly before I boarded the *Athenia*.

London was a city **frantically** preparing for war. Germany, under Adolf Hitler, had invaded Poland on September 1; an ultimatum from Great Britain's prime minister, Neville Chamberlain, was under way;

and British reserves had been called up. Children were being evacuated. Railroad terminals were jammed with people fleeing the city. The act of filling bags with sand to build protective walls was **pervasive**; activity in backyard air-raid shelters was frenetic. Still, I was reluctant to leave the country in which I had been working since leaving college in America.

After much deliberation, I decided to look into the availability of transatlantic passage home. This put me at the counter of a heavily crowded travel agency only a day before the 14,000-ton ocean liner *Athenia* was to depart from Liverpool. The fluke that landed me on board the ship was a last-minute cancellation. While standing at the ticket counter trying to make up my mind, the impatient booking agent snapped, "Do you want the ticket, or don't you? There are thousands ready to snatch it up. Besides, don't you know there's no better way to die than by drowning?"

He could not know how devastatingly close his sarcastic comment came to prophecy, for I was to spend only one night in my hastily acquired cabin. Two hundred miles off the coast of Ireland, at 7:40 p.m. on Sunday, September 3, 1939, less than 12 hours after England and France declared war on Germany, the *Athenia* was torpedoed by a Nazi submarine, the U-30. There were 1,102 passengers and a crew of 315 on board the *Athenia*. We came from all walks of life and many countries: Canada, the United States, Poland, other middle European nations, and the British Isles. Contrasts were dramatic. Sad-faced Slavic peasants with shoeless children, Texas sorority girls, middle-class professionals, and those rich enough for first-class cabins were aboard the overbooked and overcrowded ship.

S.S. *Athenia*

Some luxury liners had already been decommissioned in anticipation of war. The *Athenia*'s gymnasium had been turned into a dormitory; crew members gave some of their quarters to passengers; passengers were doubling up. Meals were scheduled for three sittings instead of the customary two.

I boarded the boat on Saturday after hastily packing and traveling north from London. On Sunday morning, I stood at the bulletin board and read a typewritten notice stating that Hitler had ignored Chamberlain's ultimatum. Great Britain and Germany were now at war! Total blackout orders were in effect: no cigarettes, matches, or lights of any kind were permitted on deck. Passengers walked outside at their own risk. A lifeboat drill was scheduled before noon.

I went to the drill, uncomfortable with the vague instructions and the fact that the lifeboat barely cleared the ship. I was a strong swimmer, but even as a child I had been terrified of drowning. Meanwhile, other passengers joked nervously about everything but the potential danger: food, crowds, the weather. "Don't worry," said Charles, another American passenger. "In another ten hours, we'll be too far out for submarines to follow. Let's celebrate at dinner."

the sinking of the *Athenia* as depicted by artist Arthur J. W. Burgess

I anticipated a happy evening. Back in my cabin, I dressed with special care to help allay my anxiety; a flashy black dress flecked with gold, thin sheer stockings, and delicate high-heeled evening sandals. The dining room was dotted with evening gowns and tuxedos. At a table nearby, someone toasted King George IV of England. Another officer assured his guests that in one more day, we should be clear of the danger zone.

A moment later my world changed forever.

There was no warning. No emergency call. No ship's bells. Just a crazy bang, an **explosion** like the slamming of an enormous steel vault bank door, and the deafening sound of a dead weight hitting the side of the ship followed by inky black and utter pandemonium. The ship lurched. Dishes crashed to the floor.

Glasses and silverware slid off the tables. The blacked-out dining room became alive with people screaming, the floor a mass of scrambling legs and feet.

I stumbled from the table toward the staircase, dragged and pushed by bodies pressed close against me. The air was filled with thick, lung-choking soot. It was still light outside when I reached the deck. A huge cloud of black smoke hung over the water. I went to the open part of the main deck. Deck chairs were overturned. People rushed helter-skelter in all directions. A **stewardess** collected blankets to take to the lifeboats. Now I could hear the screech of rusting pulleys lowering lifeboats to the water, and I rushed back to my station. Although I didn't have a life jacket, I climbed into the boat. I refused the blanket being handed out by the stewardess. Others, older and with children, needed them more. Our boat swung out, half-filled.

"Cut the cables!" yelled an officer. Our boat landed with a *posh*, and I felt the water moving underneath as we slid away from the ship's side.

I shivered in my fancy dress. Whitecapped waves rolled up against us. A high wave sent a spray of water into the boat, nearly capsizing it. Rowing grew increasingly difficult. Most of those on the oars were passengers, many of them refugees who understood little or no English. The boat was rocking more violently now. Rafts floated by. The sight of an overturned lifeboat sent shudders through everyone. Could it happen to us?

Across the black waves and the darkness came a sudden shout from another lifeboat. "Have you got a bucket? We're leaking fast." Mac, our Scottish coxswain, yelled back, "We can give you our bailer. We need the bucket ourselves. And we'll take some of your people."

The sea was too choppy for us to take on many more passengers. Two children tumbled over our bow while Mac and several other men struggled to hold the lifeboats together with their hands. Someone announced that it was 2 a.m. I could not believe it had been nearly seven hours since the explosion. The sea continued to chop and churn. The energies of everyone in the boat merged into a single effort, staying afloat.

I was scared to death, of course, yet somehow calmed by a sense of **determination**. Thinking about what I went through back then, and how (and why) I managed to survive, is actually more terrifying in some ways.

Other lights pierced the murky darkness, and the hulk of two ships loomed nearby. We rowed harder, heading for the second vessel—a slim, white yacht flying a Swedish flag.

Close to the yacht's stern, a nearly swamped lifeboat was bobbing up and down. The half-dozen frantic passengers grabbed onto our oarlocks. "Let go!" Mac yelled, but they clung on desperately and began to jump into our lifeboat. Lifelines had been thrown to us from the yacht, and at this moment, one of the men elected to make his personal bid for safety. He tried to climb up one of the lifelines. We were being dragged closer and closer under the overhanging stern. As the yacht pitched and yawed, our boat was teetering on its side at a 45-degree angle.

The next thing I knew I was in the water, surrounded by churning bodies, thrashing arms and legs. I pushed out, kicking violently, and came up alongside our boat. It had turned turtle. Someone—a woman twice my size—grabbed my neck in a desperate stranglehold. We were going down for the third time when I made my final grasp for life.

This photo of a lifeboat rescuing survivors of the *Athenia* was taken from the deck of the *City of Flint*.

I fought to the surface, cupped the woman's chin, and at last broke her stranglehold. I was free! I reached for the woman, but the waves carried her away.

Motorized lifeboats had been sent from the yacht. Their occupants were pulling aboard those they could reach. I was treading water, yelling, "Wait for me!" Suddenly two powerful arms mercifully lifted me out of the choking brine and I found myself in a lifeboat, wet, gasping, retching seawater, and covered in oil. They brought me aboard the Swedish *Southern Cross*.

Among the ships that had picked up the *Athenia*'s distress signal was the American freighter *City of Flint*. Soon crew members from the *Flint* began

survivors of the *Athenia* being brought to shore in Galway, Ireland

ferrying victims from the *Southern Cross* over to the freighter. As we neared the *Flint*, I was overjoyed to see the U.S. flag. But the sight of the long, scary ladder hanging down the freighter's side transformed joy to fear. I remembered those who had slipped between the boats the night before and the injuries many others had suffered trying to board other rescue ships or lifeboats.

I ground my teeth, determined not to look up or down. The climb was not as long as I feared. Soon strong arms pulled me over the rail onto the *City of Flint*'s deck.

I was safe aboard an American ship. My whole life lay ahead of me.

And America was not at war. Not yet.

The final count of those on the *Athenia* who died was 112, among them 69 women and 16 children. The news that the Germans had attacked an unarmed passenger vessel carrying mostly women and children sent a wave of horror around the world.

Cathleen Schurr went on to become an actress, appearing in many professional stock companies on the East Coast. She was one of the founding members of the Washington Area Feminist Theatre and co-founded and performed with the D.C.-based theater group Three's Company. She worked in films with Alan Alda and Burt Reynolds and was a featured player in Al Pacino's *... And Justice for All*. An accomplished author and poet, Ms. Schurr's credits include three books for adults, six for children (including the Golden Book classic *The Shy Little Kitten*), several books of poetry, and several bylines in the *New York Times*, the *Christian Science Monitor*, and *Family Circle* magazine.

In this photo from 1989, I am wearing the pea jacket that was given to me by a steward aboard the *Southern Cross*.

Analyze the Memoir
- Whom is the memoir about?
- What is the memoir about?
- What other people are involved in the memoir?
- This memoir includes thoughts the author had while the events were taking place. Identify two.
- This memoir includes thoughts the author has right now about what happened in the past. Identify two.
- What does the author learn from writing her memoir?
- How does the memoir end?

Focus on Comprehension: Text Structure and Organization
- The author uses description as a text structure to support information in this memoir. Identify two places where description is used. How does this text structure help you understand the author and her experience?
- Which text structure does the author use on page 9 when she finds out about Great Britain and Germany being at war?
- The author uses her senses to describe what happened after the explosion. Find examples and explain which senses she uses.

Tips for Interpreting Text Structure
- ▶ Words signaling cause and effect or problem and solution include **because**, **so**, **as a result**, **therefore**, and **consequently**.
- ▶ Words signaling comparison and contrast include **however**, **but**, **too**, **on the other hand**, and **instead**.
- ▶ Words signaling sequence or steps in a process might include specific dates, **first**, **after**, **then**, **finally**, **now**, **later**, and **not long after**.
- ▶ Words signaling description include **also**, **in fact**, **for instance**, and details and sense words.

Analyze the Tools Writers Use: Writer's Voice
- On page 10, the author says that she was uncomfortable with the vague drill instructions and that she was a strong swimmer but was afraid of drowning. What do these words tell you about the author?
- On page 13, the author says that her boat "turned turtle." How is this an example of writer's voice?
- Through the memoir, the author uses her own voice when she writes about her personal determination. Identify two examples.

Focus on Words: Suffixes

Make a chart like the one below. Read each word and identify its part of speech. Then identify the base or root word and suffix. Finally, identify the word's meaning.

Page	Word	Part of Speech	Base or Root Word	Suffix	Word Meaning
8	frantically				
8	pervasive				
11	explosion				
11	stewardess				
12	determination				

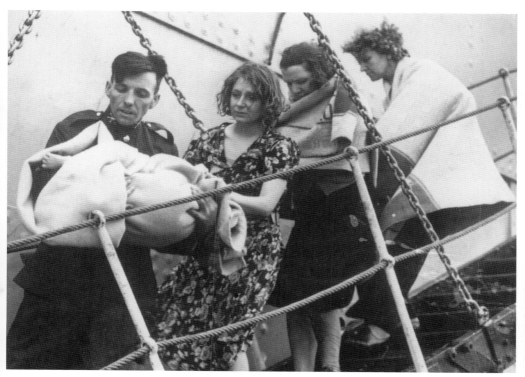

A soldier helps *Athenia* survivors to safety.

My Childhood in Wartime France

Jean-Claude (left) and m in 1944

France was divided in June 1940 after Germany invaded.

The memoir is written in the first person ("I").

"Charles, *viens ici* [Come here]!"

My friend Jean-Claude motions for me to join him. We are two six-year-old boys playing on the streets of Paulhaguet, France, a small village in the mountains south of Paris. It's not unusual for us to find something that catches our interest.

Curious, I walk over to where Jean-Claude is standing and look down. On the ground are two rifle cartridges still loaded with explosives. "*Fantastique* [fantastic]!" A treasure! He picks up the small golden bullets. We often find grenades, live ammunition, and artillery shells that have been left behind by soldiers in battle. Sometimes we even find whole rifles. It is June 1944, and World War II has been going on for five years.

"Where do you want to go?" I ask.

"The usual place," Jean-Claude says.

The usual place is a stone wall on the outskirts of the village, away from the eyes of our parents. Ready for adventure, we hurry, taking our slingshots out of our pockets as we walk. Jean-Claude hands me a bullet and keeps one. I place my bullet in the pouch of my slingshot. We both take aim, pulling back the two rubber strips on the sling as we begin to count.

"*Un! Deux! Trois!*" [One! Two! Three!]

We release our miniature catapults. The bullets fly toward the rough stone wall. *Kaboom!* The shells explode, sending up a cloud of white dust.

The memoir focuses on events the way the author remembers them.

"Let's go find some more!" I say to Jean-Claude.

We head back into the village. We know we will find additional treasures because soldiers often drop their weapons as they flee a skirmish, and the fighting has become so frequent. There are many ways a kid can make life fun during wartime.

The writer includes dialogue. It may not be what was actually said word for word, but it captures the general idea and feel of the event being described.

But the lives of many adults, including my parents, are in turmoil as the war continues to sweep across Europe.

"I never thought Nazism would happen in a country like Germany," my mother says.

My mother and father were both émigrés who had moved to Paris from Saint Petersburg, Russia, in 1918, but they had a fondness for Germany for they met as students at the Berlin University of the Arts. My father, Albrecht Hipser, was a musician, a Postimpressionist painter, and a left-wing activist. My mother, Hermina, was an intellectual freethinker and graphic artist. They often spoke German when they were together. After they finished art school, they moved back to Paris, where I was born in 1938.

As a baby, I could not know that I had been born into a world in turmoil. In Germany, Hitler was growing more and more powerful. France tried to appease the Nazis to stay out of the rising conflict, but the effort failed. In 1939, when I was one year old, Germany invaded Poland and France declared war. World War II had begun. There was heavy fighting. At the same time, Italy invaded the southern part of France and took possession. My country was now split in two.

Adolf Hitler, leader of the Nazi Party (left). A German motorcycle unit roars through Paris, France, in 1940 (above).

On June 22, 1940, France surrendered to Germany. The French were in shock. The Germans forced the French to form a new government in Vichy, a city in the center of France. This new government followed many of the most frightening policies of the Nazis. They targeted people who were deemed "undesirable." The list was long: immigrants, foreigners, Jews, Communists, Freemasons, Gypsies, homosexuals, and left-wing activists.

By now my parents were naturalized French citizens, but they still spoke with a Russian accent. They held many beliefs that were viewed with suspicion by both Germany and the new pro-German Vichy government. The German occupation in northern France was soon enforcing strict **censorship** and creating ongoing propaganda to intimidate citizens. This was a time when neighbor would turn upon neighbor, informing the authorities to come arrest anyone who might be antigovernment or "undesirable." It was a frightening time.

In the winter of 1941, my parents decided to leave Paris. My grandmother owned a house in southern France, so my mother and father packed our bags. We got on a train and went to join other family members who were already residing in Nice, a city on the Mediterranean Sea. Even though Nice was occupied by Italy at that time, it had become a city of refuge for many people who wanted to avoid both French and Nazi **persecution**. Nice was considered a "free zone."

But the war still had a devastating effect on people who lived in the region. Everything was rationed. Sometimes we would have electricity for only two or three hours a day. Mother would say, "You have to take a bath now because there won't be any water later." And there was very little food in the stores. Everyone was thin. We ate a lot of sugar beets, which are like rutabagas. I cannot look at them today without gagging. Yet once the Germans discovered they could use sugar beets to make fuel for their cars, we didn't even have those to eat anymore.

One terrible day my aunt Nora, my mother's sister, and her husband Grischa were arrested by the Vichy government

a Nazi concentration camp

militia. The reason given for their arrest was that they had a Russian-sounding last name—Sinelnikoff. (Germany had invaded Russia in 1941, so these two countries now were also at war.) Neighbors watched as they were dragged out of their house, put into a car, and driven away. People were afraid to interfere. When the neighbors saw that Aunt Nora's two children, ages four and six, had not been taken, they snuck inside and found my young cousins hiding in a closet. That's how Natasha and Costia survived. Aunt and Uncle, we learned, were sent off to Auschwitz, a concentration camp, where they died. The harshness of their tragic death juxtaposed with the near-miraculous survival of my cousins chills me to this day.

After my aunt and uncle were taken away, my parents wanted to move to a more remote spot up in the mountains. That is how I came to live in Paulhaguet, the small village where Jean-Claude and I would find the treasures left behind by the battling French, Italian, and German soldiers.

My family lived in a tall, narrow house that overlooked a winding cobblestone street. One day when I was looking out the window, I saw men with guns scrambling and running to take up positions on the street. These men were members of the rural guerrilla resistance, the Maquis. In French, *maquis* means "bush." At that time, there were **numerous** anti-German resistance movements based within France, and they were determined to fight the Nazis. My father was also a member of the **resistance** movement, but I didn't know that at the time.

Mum and I in Paulhaguet.

Suddenly a German car, a Kubelwagen, drove down the street, right by our house.

"Charles! Get away from the window!" my mother yelled. Frightened, she grabbed me, ran upstairs, and made me hide under the bed. Shots rang out, ricocheting against the buildings.

Bang! Bang! Bang! Boom!

There were shouts and cries and calls for help. Then there was silence. The Germans won this battle and rounded up many of the local people and storekeepers. This was the only firefight that I ever witnessed close up.

Food remained scarce, and I was very skinny. The shelves of the local shops were empty. People would exchange jewelry for potatoes. The Germans had taken all the butter, milk, and eggs from our village to feed their troops. My mother and I would hike far up into the mountains to try to buy food from the farmers who lived there. Once, after a very long hike, we found a group of farm women who did not speak a single word of French. I was amazed! At that time, girls in this area didn't go to school, so they had never learned the language of their country. They spoke a local dialect that sounded like a combination of Welsh and Gaelic. We needed a translator to talk to them!

D-Day: Allied troops storming Normandy beach in northwest France on June 6, 1944

Two events in 1944 had a huge impact on the rest of my life. On June 6, Allied troops invaded Normandy. This was D-Day, where 24,000 American, British, Canadian, and Free French troops began an air assault shortly after midnight. They were followed by an **amphibious** landing of Allied troops and armored divisions that morning.

the liberation of
France, 1945

The memoir includes thoughts and feelings about the events that explain why they are important to the author. He also reflects on the experience sixty years later, from his vantage point as an adult.

Now the Germans were being attacked by the Allied forces from the west while the Russians were attacking from the east. Although D-Day did not end the war, it was the beginning of the end. It would be eleven months before Germany finally surrendered.

Then, in August of that same year, my father was killed. My mother never told me the exact circumstances of his death. I wish I had pressed her for details; not knowing makes me sad, even a bit angry. But I now understand her silence. At the time, my mother was in her late thirties, a single woman facing a world at war with a six-year-old.

After my father's death, my mother moved out of the mountains and back to southern France. Because she was multilingual, she was able to find a job with the art department of the occupation forces to help during this very difficult time. She made posters that supported the military effort. We started getting better food.

One night mother came home from work with a package. It was from her American boss, and it contained useful things like combs and soap. One item in the package was a square, orange brick. It looked like a kind of soap made in France. We wet our hands, but it would not lather up. We found out later that it was Velveeta cheese, and we were supposed to eat it!

In the summer of 1945, my mother and I took a trip to Villefranche-sur-Mer, a beautiful seaside village on the French Riviera. U.S. Navy warships were in port. Germany had just surrendered. My mother wanted me to meet the American liberators, so a large group of us boarded a local fisherman's boat. It was so overcrowded that the water was half an inch from the gunwales. As I stepped on board the U.S. ship, I thought, "Someday I will move to America. Someday soon."

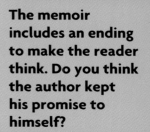

The memoir includes an ending to make the reader think. Do you think the author kept his promise to himself?

Charles Hipser moved to New York in 1960. Initially working at the ticket counter for Air France, he eventually became involved in film production. Mr. Hipser has worked as a producer, director, director of photography, and editor on numerous television commercials and corporate films, television documentaries, and public service announcements. Mr. Hipser is a recipient of the New York Film Festival bronze award for the travelogue *The World of Trafalgar*. He is currently the executive producer and owner of Evergreen Video Productions.

Reread the Memoir

Analyze the Memoir

- Whom is the memoir about?
- What is the memoir about?
- What other people are involved in the memoir?
- This memoir includes thoughts the author had while the events were taking place. Identify two.
- This memoir includes thoughts the author has right now about what happened in the past. Identify two.
- What does the author learn from writing his memoir?
- How does the memoir end?

Focus on Comprehension: Text Structure and Organization

- Locate the paragraph on page 19 that begins with "We head back into the village." This paragraph contains a cause-and-effect text structure. What cause-and-effect key word does the author use?
- Which text structure does the author use on page 20 when he tells about the world events into which he was born?
- The author uses description as a text structure to support information in this memoir. Identify two places where description is used. How does this text structure help you understand the author and his experiences?

Focus on Personal Photographs

When authors write their memoirs, they want readers to make connections with their personal stories. To do this, authors sometimes include personal photographs. Locate the personal photographs included in these two memoirs. How do these photographs help you make connections with the author?

Analyze the Tools Writers Use: Writer's Voice

- Even though the author was a young boy during wartime, he still managed to have fun. Find examples of this in the memoir.
- On pages 22–23, the author describes what happened the day his aunt and uncle were arrested by the Vichy government militia. What part of this paragraph includes an example of writer's voice?
- On page 26, the author says that he wished he'd pressed his mother on events surrounding his father's death, but now he understands her silence. How is this an example of writer's voice?

Focus on Words: Suffixes

Make a chart like the one below. Read each word and identify its part of speech. Then identify the base or root word and suffix. Finally, identify the word's meaning.

Page	Word	Part of Speech	Base or Root Word	Suffix	Word Meaning
22	censorship				
22	persecution				
24	numerous				
24	resistance				
25	amphibious				

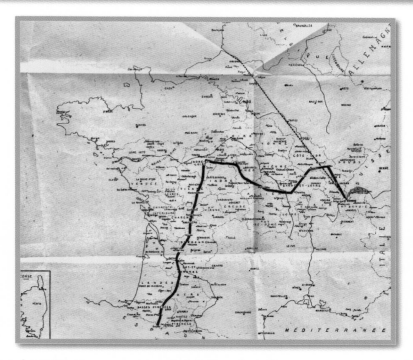

By July 1940, France was a divided nation. Germany occupied the area above the dark line, which included Paris. The pro-German Vichy government ruled over the area below the line.

How does an author write a
Memoir?

Reread "My Childhood in Wartime France," and think about what Charles Hipser did to write this memoir. How does he show how important this event was in his life? How does he make you feel as if you were there?

❶ Decide on an Important Event or Period in Your Life

Remember that a memoir is an actual retelling of something you have experienced. It allows you to relive that time and reflect upon the emotions you feel now as a type of "self-discovery." In "My Childhood in Wartime France," the author shares memories of what he did as a boy and how his family lived through the ordeal. He expresses both how he reacted to the events then and also how remembering them makes him feel today.

❷ Decide Who Else Should Be in Your Memoir

Other people often play a large part in the important events of your life. Ask yourself the following questions:
- Who was with me?
- Which people had the most impact on my experience?
- How will I describe these people?
- How did these people feel about the event?
- Did these people add to the conflict or help overcome it?

Person	Impact on Author's Experience
childhood friend Jean-Claude	helped Charles have adventures like a "normal" kid during the war
parents	because of their Russian background, the family did not feel safe in wartime France
grandmother	the house she owned in the "free zone" of Nice offered Charles and his parents a refuge from the dangerous life they faced in Paris
Aunt Nora and Uncle Grischa	their arrest by the Nazis would haunt Charles into his adult years

❸ Recall Setting and Events

Jot down notes about what happened and where it happened. Ask yourself the following questions:
- Where did the important events take place? How will I describe these places?
- What was the situation or problem I experienced? Was the experience happy, scary, sad, or surprising?
- What parts do I remember most? Why are these incidents memorable?
- How did my experience turn out?
- What questions might my readers have that I could answer in my memoir?
- What did I learn about myself from this experience? What more did I learn by writing about it?

Element of Memoir	Details	Effect on Author
Setting	France during World War II	The war made Charles and his friends find unique ways to have "normal" kid adventures.
Situation or Problem	staying safe from the Nazis and strict Vichy government	It was a frightening time.
Events	1. World War II starts when author is one year old. 2. France surrenders to Germany and is occupied; Vichy government is set up. 3. Author and friend play like normal six-year-olds. 4. Family leaves Paris for Nice to be safer. 5. Aunt and uncle taken to concentration camp; cousins hide and are saved. 6. Allied troops invade France. 7. Author's father is killed. 8. Encounters Americans who liberated France.	Is unaware of what peace is like as a young child; is frightened for his family; experiences normal childhood excitement and adventures; experiences hunger because of food rationing; is haunted for his entire life by what happened to his aunt, uncle, and cousins; sad and angry about father's death and mother's silence, but as an adult understands the challenges she faced; so influenced by the Americans that he vows to move to America as soon as he can.
How the Experience Turned Out	Author moved to New York in 1960.	Author became successful in film production.

Glossary

amphibious (am-FIH-bee-us) invaded by land, sea, and air troops at the same time (page 25)

censorship (SEN-ser-ship) the practice of limiting freedom of speech and the press (page 22)

determination (dih-ter-mih-NAY-shun) a firm intention or focused effort to achieve a desired result (page 12)

explosion (ik-SPLOH-zhun) a loud bursting (page 11)

frantically (FRAN-tik-lee) in a way that is out of control and panic-stricken (page 8)

numerous (NOO-muh-rus) many (page 24)

persecution (per-sih-KYOO-shun) the act of harassing or punishing people because they differ in background or beliefs from those in power (page 22)

pervasive (per-VAY-siv) happening all around (page 8)

resistance (rih-ZIS-tuns) opposition; an underground organization of a conquered people using secret operations to fight back (page 24)

stewardess (STOO-er-des) female employed on board to provide food and drink and attend to passengers' needs (page 11)